Vacation Rental Guest Book

Welcome!

Thank you for choosing us for your vacation.

We hope you have enjoyed your stay with us. Please share your experience with us and be sure to read through the past guests' memories and travel tips.

Wishing you the most enjoyable stay.

Signed,

Guest(s) Name:

Dates of Stay:

Is this your first stay with us?

What restaurant(s) in the area do you recommend?

What is a must see attraction in the area?

What local activities are a must?

Please share your favorite memory from this trip...

Guest(s) Name:

Dates of Stay:

Is this your first stay with us?

What restaurant(s) in the area do you recommend?

What is a must see attraction in the area?

What local activities are a must?

Please share your favorite memory from this trip...

Guest(s) Name:

Dates of Stay:

Is this your first stay with us?

What restaurant(s) in the area do you recommend?

What is a must see attraction in the area?

What local activities are a must?

Please share your favorite memory from this trip...

Guest(s) Name:

Dates of Stay:

Is this your first stay with us?

What restaurant(s) in the area do you recommend?

What is a must see attraction in the area?

What local activities are a must?

Please share your favorite memory from this trip...

Guest(s) Name:

Dates of Stay:

Is this your first stay with us?

What restaurant(s) in the area do you recommend?

What is a must see attraction in the area?

What local activities are a must?

Please share your favorite memory from this trip...

Guest(s) Name:

Dates of Stay:

Is this your first stay with us?

What restaurant(s) in the area do you recommend?

What is a must see attraction in the area?

What local activities are a must?

Please share your favorite memory from this trip...

Guest(s) Name:

Dates of Stay:

Is this your first stay with us?

What restaurant(s) in the area do you recommend?

What is a must see attraction in the area?

What local activities are a must?

Please share your favorite memory from this trip...

Guest(s) Name:

Dates of Stay:

Is this your first stay with us?

What restaurant(s) in the area do you recommend?

What is a must see attraction in the area?

What local activities are a must?

Please share your favorite memory from this trip...

Guest(s) Name:

Dates of Stay:

Is this your first stay with us?

What restaurant(s) in the area do you recommend?

What is a must see attraction in the area?

What local activities are a must?

Please share your favorite memory from this trip...

Guest(s) Name:

Dates of Stay:

Is this your first stay with us?

What restaurant(s) in the area do you recommend?

What is a must see attraction in the area?

What local activities are a must?

Please share your favorite memory from this trip...

Guest(s) Name:

Dates of Stay:

Is this your first stay with us?

What restaurant(s) in the area do you recommend?

What is a must see attraction in the area?

What local activities are a must?

Please share your favorite memory from this trip...

Guest(s) Name:

Dates of Stay:

Is this your first stay with us?

What restaurant(s) in the area do you recommend?

What is a must see attraction in the area?

What local activities are a must?

Please share your favorite memory from this trip...

Guest(s) Name:

Dates of Stay:

Is this your first stay with us?

What restaurant(s) in the area do you recommend?

What is a must see attraction in the area?

What local activities are a must?

Please share your favorite memory from this trip...

Guest(s) Name:

Dates of Stay:

Is this your first stay with us?

What restaurant(s) in the area do you recommend?

What is a must see attraction in the area?

What local activities are a must?

Please share your favorite memory from this trip...

Guest(s) Name:

Dates of Stay:

Is this your first stay with us?

What restaurant(s) in the area do you recommend?

What is a must see attraction in the area?

What local activities are a must?

Please share your favorite memory from this trip...

Guest(s) Name:

Dates of Stay:

Is this your first stay with us?

What restaurant(s) in the area do you recommend?

What is a must see attraction in the area?

What local activities are a must?

Please share your favorite memory from this trip...

Guest(s) Name:

Dates of Stay:

Is this your first stay with us?

What restaurant(s) in the area do you recommend?

What is a must see attraction in the area?

What local activities are a must?

Please share your favorite memory from this trip...

Guest(s) Name:

Dates of Stay:

Is this your first stay with us?

What restaurant(s) in the area do you recommend?

What is a must see attraction in the area?

What local activities are a must?

Please share your favorite memory from this trip...

Guest(s) Name:

Dates of Stay:

Is this your first stay with us?

What restaurant(s) in the area do you recommend?

What is a must see attraction in the area?

What local activities are a must?

Please share your favorite memory from this trip...

Guest(s) Name:

Dates of Stay:

Is this your first stay with us?

What restaurant(s) in the area do you recommend?

What is a must see attraction in the area?

What local activities are a must?

Please share your favorite memory from this trip...

Guest(s) Name:

Dates of Stay:

Is this your first stay with us?

What restaurant(s) in the area do you recommend?

What is a must see attraction in the area?

What local activities are a must?

Please share your favorite memory from this trip...

Guest(s) Name:

Dates of Stay:

Is this your first stay with us?

What restaurant(s) in the area do you recommend?

What is a must see attraction in the area?

What local activities are a must?

Please share your favorite memory from this trip...

Guest(s) Name:

Dates of Stay:

Is this your first stay with us?

What restaurant(s) in the area do you recommend?

What is a must see attraction in the area?

What local activities are a must?

Please share your favorite memory from this trip...

Guest(s) Name:

Dates of Stay:

Is this your first stay with us?

What restaurant(s) in the area do you recommend?

What is a must see attraction in the area?

What local activities are a must?

Please share your favorite memory from this trip...

Guest(s) Name:

Dates of Stay:

Is this your first stay with us?

What restaurant(s) in the area do you recommend?

What is a must see attraction in the area?

What local activities are a must?

Please share your favorite memory from this trip...

Guest(s) Name:

Dates of Stay:

Is this your first stay with us?

What restaurant(s) in the area do you recommend?

What is a must see attraction in the area?

What local activities are a must?

Please share your favorite memory from this trip...

Guest(s) Name:

Dates of Stay:

Is this your first stay with us?

What restaurant(s) in the area do you recommend?

What is a must see attraction in the area?

What local activities are a must?

Please share your favorite memory from this trip...

Guest(s) Name:

Dates of Stay:

Is this your first stay with us?

What restaurant(s) in the area do you recommend?

What is a must see attraction in the area?

What local activities are a must?

Please share your favorite memory from this trip...

Guest(s) Name:

Dates of Stay:

Is this your first stay with us?

What restaurant(s) in the area do you recommend?

What is a must see attraction in the area?

What local activities are a must?

Please share your favorite memory from this trip...

Guest(s) Name:

Dates of Stay:

Is this your first stay with us?

What restaurant(s) in the area do you recommend?

What is a must see attraction in the area?

What local activities are a must?

Please share your favorite memory from this trip...

Guest(s) Name:

Dates of Stay:

Is this your first stay with us?

What restaurant(s) in the area do you recommend?

What is a must see attraction in the area?

What local activities are a must?

Please share your favorite memory from this trip...

Guest(s) Name:

Dates of Stay:

Is this your first stay with us?

What restaurant(s) in the area do you recommend?

What is a must see attraction in the area?

What local activities are a must?

Please share your favorite memory from this trip...

Guest(s) Name:

Dates of Stay:

Is this your first stay with us?

What restaurant(s) in the area do you recommend?

What is a must see attraction in the area?

What local activities are a must?

Please share your favorite memory from this trip...

Guest(s) Name:

Dates of Stay:

Is this your first stay with us?

What restaurant(s) in the area do you recommend?

What is a must see attraction in the area?

What local activities are a must?

Please share your favorite memory from this trip...

Guest(s) Name:

Dates of Stay:

Is this your first stay with us?

What restaurant(s) in the area do you recommend?

What is a must see attraction in the area?

What local activities are a must?

Please share your favorite memory from this trip...

Guest(s) Name:

Dates of Stay:

Is this your first stay with us?

What restaurant(s) in the area do you recommend?

What is a must see attraction in the area?

What local activities are a must?

Please share your favorite memory from this trip...

Guest(s) Name:

Dates of Stay:

Is this your first stay with us?

What restaurant(s) in the area do you recommend?

What is a must see attraction in the area?

What local activities are a must?

Please share your favorite memory from this trip...

Guest(s) Name:

Dates of Stay:

Is this your first stay with us?

What restaurant(s) in the area do you recommend?

What is a must see attraction in the area?

What local activities are a must?

Please share your favorite memory from this trip...

Guest(s) Name:

Dates of Stay:

Is this your first stay with us?

What restaurant(s) in the area do you recommend?

What is a must see attraction in the area?

What local activities are a must?

Please share your favorite memory from this trip...

Guest(s) Name:

Dates of Stay:

Is this your first stay with us?

What restaurant(s) in the area do you recommend?

What is a must see attraction in the area?

What local activities are a must?

Please share your favorite memory from this trip...

Guest(s) Name:

Dates of Stay:

Is this your first stay with us?

What restaurant(s) in the area do you recommend?

What is a must see attraction in the area?

What local activities are a must?

Please share your favorite memory from this trip...

Guest(s) Name:

Dates of Stay:

Is this your first stay with us?

What restaurant(s) in the area do you recommend?

What is a must see attraction in the area?

What local activities are a must?

Please share your favorite memory from this trip...

Guest(s) Name:

Dates of Stay:

Is this your first stay with us?

What restaurant(s) in the area do you recommend?

What is a must see attraction in the area?

What local activities are a must?

Please share your favorite memory from this trip...

Guest(s) Name:

Dates of Stay:

Is this your first stay with us?

What restaurant(s) in the area do you recommend?

What is a must see attraction in the area?

What local activities are a must?

Please share your favorite memory from this trip...

Guest(s) Name:

Dates of Stay:

Is this your first stay with us?

What restaurant(s) in the area do you recommend?

What is a must see attraction in the area?

What local activities are a must?

Please share your favorite memory from this trip...

Guest(s) Name:

Dates of Stay:

Is this your first stay with us?

What restaurant(s) in the area do you recommend?

What is a must see attraction in the area?

What local activities are a must?

Please share your favorite memory from this trip...

Guest(s) Name:

Dates of Stay:

Is this your first stay with us?

What restaurant(s) in the area do you recommend?

What is a must see attraction in the area?

What local activities are a must?

Please share your favorite memory from this trip...

Guest(s) Name:

Dates of Stay:

Is this your first stay with us?

What restaurant(s) in the area do you recommend?

What is a must see attraction in the area?

What local activities are a must?

Please share your favorite memory from this trip...

Guest(s) Name:

Dates of Stay:

Is this your first stay with us?

What restaurant(s) in the area do you recommend?

What is a must see attraction in the area?

What local activities are a must?

Please share your favorite memory from this trip...

Guest(s) Name:

Dates of Stay:

Is this your first stay with us?

What restaurant(s) in the area do you recommend?

What is a must see attraction in the area?

What local activities are a must?

Please share your favorite memory from this trip...

Guest(s) Name:

Dates of Stay:

Is this your first stay with us?

What restaurant(s) in the area do you recommend?

What is a must see attraction in the area?

What local activities are a must?

Please share your favorite memory from this trip...

Guest(s) Name:

Dates of Stay:

Is this your first stay with us?

What restaurant(s) in the area do you recommend?

What is a must see attraction in the area?

What local activities are a must?

Please share your favorite memory from this trip...

Guest(s) Name:

Dates of Stay:

Is this your first stay with us?

What restaurant(s) in the area do you recommend?

What is a must see attraction in the area?

What local activities are a must?

Please share your favorite memory from this trip...

Guest(s) Name:

Dates of Stay:

Is this your first stay with us?

What restaurant(s) in the area do you recommend?

What is a must see attraction in the area?

What local activities are a must?

Please share your favorite memory from this trip...

Guest(s) Name:

Dates of Stay:

Is this your first stay with us?

What restaurant(s) in the area do you recommend?

What is a must see attraction in the area?

What local activities are a must?

Please share your favorite memory from this trip...

Guest(s) Name:

Dates of Stay:

Is this your first stay with us?

What restaurant(s) in the area do you recommend?

What is a must see attraction in the area?

What local activities are a must?

Please share your favorite memory from this trip...

Guest(s) Name:

Dates of Stay:

Is this your first stay with us?

What restaurant(s) in the area do you recommend?

What is a must see attraction in the area?

What local activities are a must?

Please share your favorite memory from this trip...

Guest(s) Name:

Dates of Stay:

Is this your first stay with us?

What restaurant(s) in the area do you recommend?

What is a must see attraction in the area?

What local activities are a must?

Please share your favorite memory from this trip...

Guest(s) Name:

Dates of Stay:

Is this your first stay with us?

What restaurant(s) in the area do you recommend?

What is a must see attraction in the area?

What local activities are a must?

Please share your favorite memory from this trip...

Guest(s) Name:

Dates of Stay:

Is this your first stay with us?

What restaurant(s) in the area do you recommend?

What is a must see attraction in the area?

What local activities are a must?

Please share your favorite memory from this trip...

Guest(s) Name:

Dates of Stay:

Is this your first stay with us?

What restaurant(s) in the area do you recommend?

What is a must see attraction in the area?

What local activities are a must?

Please share your favorite memory from this trip...

Guest(s) Name:

Dates of Stay:

Is this your first stay with us?

What restaurant(s) in the area do you recommend?

What is a must see attraction in the area?

What local activities are a must?

Please share your favorite memory from this trip...

Guest(s) Name:

Dates of Stay:

Is this your first stay with us?

What restaurant(s) in the area do you recommend?

What is a must see attraction in the area?

What local activities are a must?

Please share your favorite memory from this trip...

Guest(s) Name:

Dates of Stay:

Is this your first stay with us?

What restaurant(s) in the area do you recommend?

What is a must see attraction in the area?

What local activities are a must?

Please share your favorite memory from this trip...

Guest(s) Name:

Dates of Stay:

Is this your first stay with us?

What restaurant(s) in the area do you recommend?

What is a must see attraction in the area?

What local activities are a must?

Please share your favorite memory from this trip...

Guest(s) Name:

Dates of Stay:

Is this your first stay with us?

What restaurant(s) in the area do you recommend?

What is a must see attraction in the area?

What local activities are a must?

Please share your favorite memory from this trip...

Guest(s) Name:

Dates of Stay:

Is this your first stay with us?

What restaurant(s) in the area do you recommend?

What is a must see attraction in the area?

What local activities are a must?

Please share your favorite memory from this trip...

Guest(s) Name:

Dates of Stay:

Is this your first stay with us?

What restaurant(s) in the area do you recommend?

What is a must see attraction in the area?

What local activities are a must?

Please share your favorite memory from this trip...

Guest(s) Name:

Dates of Stay:

Is this your first stay with us?

What restaurant(s) in the area do you recommend?

What is a must see attraction in the area?

What local activities are a must?

Please share your favorite memory from this trip...

Guest(s) Name:

Dates of Stay:

Is this your first stay with us?

What restaurant(s) in the area do you recommend?

What is a must see attraction in the area?

What local activities are a must?

Please share your favorite memory from this trip...

Guest(s) Name:

Dates of Stay:

Is this your first stay with us?

What restaurant(s) in the area do you recommend?

What is a must see attraction in the area?

What local activities are a must?

Please share your favorite memory from this trip...

Guest(s) Name:

Dates of Stay:

Is this your first stay with us?

What restaurant(s) in the area do you recommend?

What is a must see attraction in the area?

What local activities are a must?

Please share your favorite memory from this trip...

Guest(s) Name:

Dates of Stay:

Is this your first stay with us?

What restaurant(s) in the area do you recommend?

What is a must see attraction in the area?

What local activities are a must?

Please share your favorite memory from this trip...

Guest(s) Name:

Dates of Stay:

Is this your first stay with us?

What restaurant(s) in the area do you recommend?

What is a must see attraction in the area?

What local activities are a must?

Please share your favorite memory from this trip...

Guest(s) Name:

Dates of Stay:

Is this your first stay with us?

What restaurant(s) in the area do you recommend?

What is a must see attraction in the area?

What local activities are a must?

Please share your favorite memory from this trip...

Guest(s) Name:

Dates of Stay:

Is this your first stay with us?

What restaurant(s) in the area do you recommend?

What is a must see attraction in the area?

What local activities are a must?

Please share your favorite memory from this trip...

Guest(s) Name:

Dates of Stay:

Is this your first stay with us?

What restaurant(s) in the area do you recommend?

What is a must see attraction in the area?

What local activities are a must?

Please share your favorite memory from this trip...

Guest(s) Name:

Dates of Stay:

Is this your first stay with us?

What restaurant(s) in the area do you recommend?

What is a must see attraction in the area?

What local activities are a must?

Please share your favorite memory from this trip...

Guest(s) Name:

Dates of Stay:

Is this your first stay with us?

What restaurant(s) in the area do you recommend?

What is a must see attraction in the area?

What local activities are a must?

Please share your favorite memory from this trip...

Guest(s) Name:

Dates of Stay:

Is this your first stay with us?

What restaurant(s) in the area do you recommend?

What is a must see attraction in the area?

What local activities are a must?

Please share your favorite memory from this trip...

Guest(s) Name:

Dates of Stay:

Is this your first stay with us?

What restaurant(s) in the area do you recommend?

What is a must see attraction in the area?

What local activities are a must?

Please share your favorite memory from this trip...

Guest(s) Name:

Dates of Stay:

Is this your first stay with us?

What restaurant(s) in the area do you recommend?

What is a must see attraction in the area?

What local activities are a must?

Please share your favorite memory from this trip...

Guest(s) Name:

Dates of Stay:

Is this your first stay with us?

What restaurant(s) in the area do you recommend?

What is a must see attraction in the area?

What local activities are a must?

Please share your favorite memory from this trip...

Guest(s) Name:

Dates of Stay:

Is this your first stay with us?

What restaurant(s) in the area do you recommend?

What is a must see attraction in the area?

What local activities are a must?

Please share your favorite memory from this trip...

Guest(s) Name:

Dates of Stay:

Is this your first stay with us?

What restaurant(s) in the area do you recommend?

What is a must see attraction in the area?

What local activities are a must?

Please share your favorite memory from this trip...

Guest(s) Name:

Dates of Stay:

Is this your first stay with us?

What restaurant(s) in the area do you recommend?

What is a must see attraction in the area?

What local activities are a must?

Please share your favorite memory from this trip...

Guest(s) Name:

Dates of Stay:

Is this your first stay with us?

What restaurant(s) in the area do you recommend?

What is a must see attraction in the area?

What local activities are a must?

Please share your favorite memory from this trip...

Guest(s) Name:

Dates of Stay:

Is this your first stay with us?

What restaurant(s) in the area do you recommend?

What is a must see attraction in the area?

What local activities are a must?

Please share your favorite memory from this trip...

Guest(s) Name:

Dates of Stay:

Is this your first stay with us?

What restaurant(s) in the area do you recommend?

What is a must see attraction in the area?

What local activities are a must?

Please share your favorite memory from this trip...

Guest(s) Name:

Dates of Stay:

Is this your first stay with us?

What restaurant(s) in the area do you recommend?

What is a must see attraction in the area?

What local activities are a must?

Please share your favorite memory from this trip...

Guest(s) Name:

Dates of Stay:

Is this your first stay with us?

What restaurant(s) in the area do you recommend?

What is a must see attraction in the area?

What local activities are a must?

Please share your favorite memory from this trip...

Guest(s) Name:

Dates of Stay:

Is this your first stay with us?

What restaurant(s) in the area do you recommend?

What is a must see attraction in the area?

What local activities are a must?

Please share your favorite memory from this trip...

Guest(s) Name:

Dates of Stay:

Is this your first stay with us?

What restaurant(s) in the area do you recommend?

What is a must see attraction in the area?

What local activities are a must?

Please share your favorite memory from this trip...

Guest(s) Name:

Dates of Stay:

Is this your first stay with us?

What restaurant(s) in the area do you recommend?

What is a must see attraction in the area?

What local activities are a must?

Please share your favorite memory from this trip...

Guest(s) Name:

Dates of Stay:

Is this your first stay with us?

What restaurant(s) in the area do you recommend?

What is a must see attraction in the area?

What local activities are a must?

Please share your favorite memory from this trip...

Guest(s) Name:

Dates of Stay:

Is this your first stay with us?

What restaurant(s) in the area do you recommend?

What is a must see attraction in the area?

What local activities are a must?

Please share your favorite memory from this trip...

Guest(s) Name:

Dates of Stay:

Is this your first stay with us?

What restaurant(s) in the area do you recommend?

What is a must see attraction in the area?

What local activities are a must?

Please share your favorite memory from this trip...

Guest(s) Name:

Dates of Stay:

Is this your first stay with us?

What restaurant(s) in the area do you recommend?

What is a must see attraction in the area?

What local activities are a must?

Please share your favorite memory from this trip...

Guest(s) Name:

Dates of Stay:

Is this your first stay with us?

What restaurant(s) in the area do you recommend?

What is a must see attraction in the area?

What local activities are a must?

Please share your favorite memory from this trip...

Guest(s) Name:

Dates of Stay:

Is this your first stay with us?

What restaurant(s) in the area do you recommend?

What is a must see attraction in the area?

What local activities are a must?

Please share your favorite memory from this trip...

Guest(s) Name:

Dates of Stay:

Is this your first stay with us?

What restaurant(s) in the area do you recommend?

What is a must see attraction in the area?

What local activities are a must?

Please share your favorite memory from this trip...

Guest(s) Name:

Dates of Stay:

Is this your first stay with us?

What restaurant(s) in the area do you recommend?

What is a must see attraction in the area?

What local activities are a must?

Please share your favorite memory from this trip...

Guest(s) Name:

Dates of Stay:

Is this your first stay with us?

What restaurant(s) in the area do you recommend?

What is a must see attraction in the area?

What local activities are a must?

Please share your favorite memory from this trip...

Guest(s) Name:

Dates of Stay:

Is this your first stay with us?

What restaurant(s) in the area do you recommend?

What is a must see attraction in the area?

What local activities are a must?

Please share your favorite memory from this trip...

Guest(s) Name:

Dates of Stay:

Is this your first stay with us?

What restaurant(s) in the area do you recommend?

What is a must see attraction in the area?

What local activities are a must?

Please share your favorite memory from this trip...

Guest(s) Name:

Dates of Stay:

Is this your first stay with us?

What restaurant(s) in the area do you recommend?

What is a must see attraction in the area?

What local activities are a must?

Please share your favorite memory from this trip...

Guest(s) Name:

Dates of Stay:

Is this your first stay with us?

What restaurant(s) in the area do you recommend?

What is a must see attraction in the area?

What local activities are a must?

Please share your favorite memory from this trip...

Guest(s) Name:

Dates of Stay:

Is this your first stay with us?

What restaurant(s) in the area do you recommend?

What is a must see attraction in the area?

What local activities are a must?

Please share your favorite memory from this trip...

Guest(s) Name:

Dates of Stay:

Is this your first stay with us?

What restaurant(s) in the area do you recommend?

What is a must see attraction in the area?

What local activities are a must?

Please share your favorite memory from this trip...

Guest(s) Name:

Dates of Stay:

Is this your first stay with us?

What restaurant(s) in the area do you recommend?

What is a must see attraction in the area?

What local activities are a must?

Please share your favorite memory from this trip...

Guest(s) Name:

Dates of Stay:

Is this your first stay with us?

What restaurant(s) in the area do you recommend?

What is a must see attraction in the area?

What local activities are a must?

Please share your favorite memory from this trip...

Guest(s) Name:

Dates of Stay:

Is this your first stay with us?

What restaurant(s) in the area do you recommend?

What is a must see attraction in the area?

What local activities are a must?

Please share your favorite memory from this trip...

Guest(s) Name:

Dates of Stay:

Is this your first stay with us?

What restaurant(s) in the area do you recommend?

What is a must see attraction in the area?

What local activities are a must?

Please share your favorite memory from this trip...

Guest(s) Name:

Dates of Stay:

Is this your first stay with us?

What restaurant(s) in the area do you recommend?

What is a must see attraction in the area?

What local activities are a must?

Please share your favorite memory from this trip...

Guest(s) Name:

Dates of Stay:

Is this your first stay with us?

What restaurant(s) in the area do you recommend?

What is a must see attraction in the area?

What local activities are a must?

Please share your favorite memory from this trip...

Guest(s) Name:

Dates of Stay:

Is this your first stay with us?

What restaurant(s) in the area do you recommend?

What is a must see attraction in the area?

What local activities are a must?

Please share your favorite memory from this trip...

Guest(s) Name:

Dates of Stay:

Is this your first stay with us?

What restaurant(s) in the area do you recommend?

What is a must see attraction in the area?

What local activities are a must?

Please share your favorite memory from this trip...

Guest(s) Name:

Dates of Stay:

Is this your first stay with us?

What restaurant(s) in the area do you recommend?

What is a must see attraction in the area?

What local activities are a must?

Please share your favorite memory from this trip...

Guest(s) Name:

Dates of Stay:

Is this your first stay with us?

What restaurant(s) in the area do you recommend?

What is a must see attraction in the area?

What local activities are a must?

Please share your favorite memory from this trip...

Guest(s) Name:

Dates of Stay:

Is this your first stay with us?

What restaurant(s) in the area do you recommend?

What is a must see attraction in the area?

What local activities are a must?

Please share your favorite memory from this trip...

Guest(s) Name:

Dates of Stay:

Is this your first stay with us?

What restaurant(s) in the area do you recommend?

What is a must see attraction in the area?

What local activities are a must?

Please share your favorite memory from this trip...

Guest(s) Name:

Dates of Stay:

Is this your first stay with us?

What restaurant(s) in the area do you recommend?

What is a must see attraction in the area?

What local activities are a must?

Please share your favorite memory from this trip...

Guest(s) Name:

Dates of Stay:

Is this your first stay with us?

What restaurant(s) in the area do you recommend?

What is a must see attraction in the area?

What local activities are a must?

Please share your favorite memory from this trip...

Guest(s) Name:

Dates of Stay:

Is this your first stay with us?

What restaurant(s) in the area do you recommend?

What is a must see attraction in the area?

What local activities are a must?

Please share your favorite memory from this trip...

Guest(s) Name:

Dates of Stay:

Is this your first stay with us?

What restaurant(s) in the area do you recommend?

What is a must see attraction in the area?

What local activities are a must?

Please share your favorite memory from this trip...

Guest(s) Name:

Dates of Stay:

Is this your first stay with us?

What restaurant(s) in the area do you recommend?

What is a must see attraction in the area?

What local activities are a must?

Please share your favorite memory from this trip...

Guest(s) Name:

Dates of Stay:

Is this your first stay with us?

What restaurant(s) in the area do you recommend?

What is a must see attraction in the area?

What local activities are a must?

Please share your favorite memory from this trip...

Guest(s) Name:

Dates of Stay:

Is this your first stay with us?

What restaurant(s) in the area do you recommend?

What is a must see attraction in the area?

What local activities are a must?

Please share your favorite memory from this trip...

Guest(s) Name:

Dates of Stay:

Is this your first stay with us?

What restaurant(s) in the area do you recommend?

What is a must see attraction in the area?

What local activities are a must?

Please share your favorite memory from this trip...

Guest(s) Name:

Dates of Stay:

Is this your first stay with us?

What restaurant(s) in the area do you recommend?

What is a must see attraction in the area?

What local activities are a must?

Please share your favorite memory from this trip...

Guest(s) Name:

Dates of Stay:

Is this your first stay with us?

What restaurant(s) in the area do you recommend?

What is a must see attraction in the area?

What local activities are a must?

Please share your favorite memory from this trip...

Guest(s) Name:

Dates of Stay:

Is this your first stay with us?

What restaurant(s) in the area do you recommend?

What is a must see attraction in the area?

What local activities are a must?

Please share your favorite memory from this trip...

Guest(s) Name:

Dates of Stay:

Is this your first stay with us?

What restaurant(s) in the area do you recommend?

What is a must see attraction in the area?

What local activities are a must?

Please share your favorite memory from this trip...

Guest(s) Name:

Dates of Stay:

Is this your first stay with us?

What restaurant(s) in the area do you recommend?

What is a must see attraction in the area?

What local activities are a must?

Please share your favorite memory from this trip...

Guest(s) Name:

Dates of Stay:

Is this your first stay with us?

What restaurant(s) in the area do you recommend?

What is a must see attraction in the area?

What local activities are a must?

Please share your favorite memory from this trip...

Guest(s) Name:

Dates of Stay:

Is this your first stay with us?

What restaurant(s) in the area do you recommend?

What is a must see attraction in the area?

What local activities are a must?

Please share your favorite memory from this trip...

Guest(s) Name:

Dates of Stay:

Is this your first stay with us?

What restaurant(s) in the area do you recommend?

What is a must see attraction in the area?

What local activities are a must?

Please share your favorite memory from this trip...

Guest(s) Name:

Dates of Stay:

Is this your first stay with us?

What restaurant(s) in the area do you recommend?

What is a must see attraction in the area?

What local activities are a must?

Please share your favorite memory from this trip...

Guest(s) Name:

Dates of Stay:

Is this your first stay with us?

What restaurant(s) in the area do you recommend?

What is a must see attraction in the area?

What local activities are a must?

Please share your favorite memory from this trip...

Guest(s) Name:

Dates of Stay:

Is this your first stay with us?

What restaurant(s) in the area do you recommend?

What is a must see attraction in the area?

What local activities are a must?

Please share your favorite memory from this trip...

Guest(s) Name:

Dates of Stay:

Is this your first stay with us?

What restaurant(s) in the area do you recommend?

What is a must see attraction in the area?

What local activities are a must?

Please share your favorite memory from this trip...

Guest(s) Name:

Dates of Stay:

Is this your first stay with us?

What restaurant(s) in the area do you recommend?

What is a must see attraction in the area?

What local activities are a must?

Please share your favorite memory from this trip...

Guest(s) Name:

Dates of Stay:

Is this your first stay with us?

What restaurant(s) in the area do you recommend?

What is a must see attraction in the area?

What local activities are a must?

Please share your favorite memory from this trip...

Guest(s) Name:

Dates of Stay:

Is this your first stay with us?

What restaurant(s) in the area do you recommend?

What is a must see attraction in the area?

What local activities are a must?

Please share your favorite memory from this trip...

Guest(s) Name:

Dates of Stay:

Is this your first stay with us?

What restaurant(s) in the area do you recommend?

What is a must see attraction in the area?

What local activities are a must?

Please share your favorite memory from this trip...

Guest(s) Name:

Dates of Stay:

Is this your first stay with us?

What restaurant(s) in the area do you recommend?

What is a must see attraction in the area?

What local activities are a must?

Please share your favorite memory from this trip...

Guest(s) Name:

Dates of Stay:

Is this your first stay with us?

What restaurant(s) in the area do you recommend?

What is a must see attraction in the area?

What local activities are a must?

Please share your favorite memory from this trip...

Guest(s) Name:

Dates of Stay:

Is this your first stay with us?

What restaurant(s) in the area do you recommend?

What is a must see attraction in the area?

What local activities are a must?

Please share your favorite memory from this trip...

Guest(s) Name:

Dates of Stay:

Is this your first stay with us?

What restaurant(s) in the area do you recommend?

What is a must see attraction in the area?

What local activities are a must?

Please share your favorite memory from this trip...

Guest(s) Name:

Dates of Stay:

Is this your first stay with us?

What restaurant(s) in the area do you recommend?

What is a must see attraction in the area?

What local activities are a must?

Please share your favorite memory from this trip...

Guest(s) Name:

Dates of Stay:

Is this your first stay with us?

What restaurant(s) in the area do you recommend?

What is a must see attraction in the area?

What local activities are a must?

Please share your favorite memory from this trip...

Guest(s) Name:

Dates of Stay:

Is this your first stay with us?

What restaurant(s) in the area do you recommend?

What is a must see attraction in the area?

What local activities are a must?

Please share your favorite memory from this trip...

Guest(s) Name:

Dates of Stay:

Is this your first stay with us?

What restaurant(s) in the area do you recommend?

What is a must see attraction in the area?

What local activities are a must?

Please share your favorite memory from this trip...

Guest(s) Name:

Dates of Stay:

Is this your first stay with us?

What restaurant(s) in the area do you recommend?

What is a must see attraction in the area?

What local activities are a must?

Please share your favorite memory from this trip...

Guest(s) Name:

Dates of Stay:

Is this your first stay with us?

What restaurant(s) in the area do you recommend?

What is a must see attraction in the area?

What local activities are a must?

Please share your favorite memory from this trip...

Guest(s) Name:

Dates of Stay:

Is this your first stay with us?

What restaurant(s) in the area do you recommend?

What is a must see attraction in the area?

What local activities are a must?

Please share your favorite memory from this trip...

Guest(s) Name:

Dates of Stay:

Is this your first stay with us?

What restaurant(s) in the area do you recommend?

What is a must see attraction in the area?

What local activities are a must?

Please share your favorite memory from this trip...

Guest(s) Name:

Dates of Stay:

Is this your first stay with us?

What restaurant(s) in the area do you recommend?

What is a must see attraction in the area?

What local activities are a must?

Please share your favorite memory from this trip...

Guest(s) Name:

Dates of Stay:

Is this your first stay with us?

What restaurant(s) in the area do you recommend?

What is a must see attraction in the area?

What local activities are a must?

Please share your favorite memory from this trip...

Guest(s) Name:

Dates of Stay:

Is this your first stay with us?

What restaurant(s) in the area do you recommend?

What is a must see attraction in the area?

What local activities are a must?

Please share your favorite memory from this trip...

Guest(s) Name:

Dates of Stay:

Is this your first stay with us?

What restaurant(s) in the area do you recommend?

What is a must see attraction in the area?

What local activities are a must?

Please share your favorite memory from this trip...

Guest(s) Name:

Dates of Stay:

Is this your first stay with us?

What restaurant(s) in the area do you recommend?

What is a must see attraction in the area?

What local activities are a must?

Please share your favorite memory from this trip...

Guest(s) Name:

Dates of Stay:

Is this your first stay with us?

What restaurant(s) in the area do you recommend?

What is a must see attraction in the area?

What local activities are a must?

Please share your favorite memory from this trip...

Guest(s) Name:

Dates of Stay:

Is this your first stay with us?

What restaurant(s) in the area do you recommend?

What is a must see attraction in the area?

What local activities are a must?

Please share your favorite memory from this trip...

Guest(s) Name:

Dates of Stay:

Is this your first stay with us?

What restaurant(s) in the area do you recommend?

What is a must see attraction in the area?

What local activities are a must?

Please share your favorite memory from this trip...

Guest(s) Name:

Dates of Stay:

Is this your first stay with us?

What restaurant(s) in the area do you recommend?

What is a must see attraction in the area?

What local activities are a must?

Please share your favorite memory from this trip...

Guest(s) Name:

Dates of Stay:

Is this your first stay with us?

What restaurant(s) in the area do you recommend?

What is a must see attraction in the area?

What local activities are a must?

Please share your favorite memory from this trip...

Guest(s) Name:

Dates of Stay:

Is this your first stay with us?

What restaurant(s) in the area do you recommend?

What is a must see attraction in the area?

What local activities are a must?

Please share your favorite memory from this trip...

Guest(s) Name:

Dates of Stay:

Is this your first stay with us?

What restaurant(s) in the area do you recommend?

What is a must see attraction in the area?

What local activities are a must?

Please share your favorite memory from this trip...

Guest(s) Name:

Dates of Stay:

Is this your first stay with us?

What restaurant(s) in the area do you recommend?

What is a must see attraction in the area?

What local activities are a must?

Please share your favorite memory from this trip...

Guest(s) Name:

Dates of Stay:

Is this your first stay with us?

What restaurant(s) in the area do you recommend?

What is a must see attraction in the area?

What local activities are a must?

Please share your favorite memory from this trip...

Guest(s) Name:

Dates of Stay:

Is this your first stay with us?

What restaurant(s) in the area do you recommend?

What is a must see attraction in the area?

What local activities are a must?

Please share your favorite memory from this trip...

Guest(s) Name:

Dates of Stay:

Is this your first stay with us?

What restaurant(s) in the area do you recommend?

What is a must see attraction in the area?

What local activities are a must?

Please share your favorite memory from this trip...

Guest(s) Name:

Dates of Stay:

Is this your first stay with us?

What restaurant(s) in the area do you recommend?

What is a must see attraction in the area?

What local activities are a must?

Please share your favorite memory from this trip...

Guest(s) Name:

Dates of Stay:

Is this your first stay with us?

What restaurant(s) in the area do you recommend?

What is a must see attraction in the area?

What local activities are a must?

Please share your favorite memory from this trip...

Guest(s) Name:

Dates of Stay:

Is this your first stay with us?

What restaurant(s) in the area do you recommend?

What is a must see attraction in the area?

What local activities are a must?

Please share your favorite memory from this trip...

Guest(s) Name:

Dates of Stay:

Is this your first stay with us?

What restaurant(s) in the area do you recommend?

What is a must see attraction in the area?

What local activities are a must?

Please share your favorite memory from this trip...

Guest(s) Name:

Dates of Stay:

Is this your first stay with us?

What restaurant(s) in the area do you recommend?

What is a must see attraction in the area?

What local activities are a must?

Please share your favorite memory from this trip...

Guest(s) Name:

Dates of Stay:

Is this your first stay with us?

What restaurant(s) in the area do you recommend?

What is a must see attraction in the area?

What local activities are a must?

Please share your favorite memory from this trip...

Guest(s) Name:

Dates of Stay:

Is this your first stay with us?

What restaurant(s) in the area do you recommend?

What is a must see attraction in the area?

What local activities are a must?

Please share your favorite memory from this trip...

Guest(s) Name:

Dates of Stay:

Is this your first stay with us?

What restaurant(s) in the area do you recommend?

What is a must see attraction in the area?

What local activities are a must?

Please share your favorite memory from this trip...

Guest(s) Name:

Dates of Stay:

Is this your first stay with us?

What restaurant(s) in the area do you recommend?

What is a must see attraction in the area?

What local activities are a must?

Please share your favorite memory from this trip...

Guest(s) Name:

Dates of Stay:

Is this your first stay with us?

What restaurant(s) in the area do you recommend?

What is a must see attraction in the area?

What local activities are a must?

Please share your favorite memory from this trip...

Guest(s) Name:

Dates of Stay:

Is this your first stay with us?

What restaurant(s) in the area do you recommend?

What is a must see attraction in the area?

What local activities are a must?

Please share your favorite memory from this trip...

Guest(s) Name:

Dates of Stay:

Is this your first stay with us?

What restaurant(s) in the area do you recommend?

What is a must see attraction in the area?

What local activities are a must?

Please share your favorite memory from this trip...

Guest(s) Name:

Dates of Stay:

Is this your first stay with us?

What restaurant(s) in the area do you recommend?

What is a must see attraction in the area?

What local activities are a must?

Please share your favorite memory from this trip...

Guest(s) Name:

Dates of Stay:

Is this your first stay with us?

What restaurant(s) in the area do you recommend?

What is a must see attraction in the area?

What local activities are a must?

Please share your favorite memory from this trip...

Guest(s) Name:

Dates of Stay:

Is this your first stay with us?

What restaurant(s) in the area do you recommend?

What is a must see attraction in the area?

What local activities are a must?

Please share your favorite memory from this trip...

Guest(s) Name:

Dates of Stay:

Is this your first stay with us?

What restaurant(s) in the area do you recommend?

What is a must see attraction in the area?

What local activities are a must?

Please share your favorite memory from this trip...

Guest(s) Name:

Dates of Stay:

Is this your first stay with us?

What restaurant(s) in the area do you recommend?

What is a must see attraction in the area?

What local activities are a must?

Please share your favorite memory from this trip...

Guest(s) Name:

Dates of Stay:

Is this your first stay with us?

What restaurant(s) in the area do you recommend?

What is a must see attraction in the area?

What local activities are a must?

Please share your favorite memory from this trip...

Guest(s) Name:

Dates of Stay:

Is this your first stay with us?

What restaurant(s) in the area do you recommend?

What is a must see attraction in the area?

What local activities are a must?

Please share your favorite memory from this trip...

Guest(s) Name:

Dates of Stay:

Is this your first stay with us?

What restaurant(s) in the area do you recommend?

What is a must see attraction in the area?

What local activities are a must?

Please share your favorite memory from this trip...

Guest(s) Name:

Dates of Stay:

Is this your first stay with us?

What restaurant(s) in the area do you recommend?

What is a must see attraction in the area?

What local activities are a must?

Please share your favorite memory from this trip...

Guest(s) Name:

Dates of Stay:

Is this your first stay with us?

What restaurant(s) in the area do you recommend?

What is a must see attraction in the area?

What local activities are a must?

Please share your favorite memory from this trip...

Guest(s) Name:

Dates of Stay:

Is this your first stay with us?

What restaurant(s) in the area do you recommend?

What is a must see attraction in the area?

What local activities are a must?

Please share your favorite memory from this trip...

Guest(s) Name:

Dates of Stay:

Is this your first stay with us?

What restaurant(s) in the area do you recommend?

What is a must see attraction in the area?

What local activities are a must?

Please share your favorite memory from this trip...

Made in the USA
Las Vegas, NV
22 October 2021